For those moments that bring us to the point where it feels like every sob is pulling your very soul out of its shell, those moments that hurt so bad that it makes you want to stop breathing…

…that is where we find our muse, our inspiration.

EMOTION CORROSION

... POETRY FROM A DISTURBED MIND ...

LEIGH HADDINGTON

TOMBTOME PUBLISHERS

FOREWORD

I started to write poetry after I began writing my first novel. It seemed like a simple way to understand how to structure ideas and patterns together. I would put pictures to them and put them onto Twitter and Instagram, and if I had owned the images I think they would have been in the book with the poems, but I don't, so I can't.

At first, every poem was shit, but I enjoyed doing them, for example:

These roses are red,
they used to be white.
You're dead on the floor,
I best take flight.

Now, I liked that even I could see that were very weak. So I kept on and wrote more, and kept going. It took a while, but soon I realised it was more about just playing with ideas and words. I could take a snapshot out of a moment or an idea and flash you an image. To me, that is what poetry is about, polaroids scattered all over a floor, showing a story or feeling.

So, here is my first photo album of a depressed, disturbed, emotional journey of 2020. It's not the prettiest of images, but its photos of my mind and experiences snatched from a window of time.

PART I
DEPRESSION

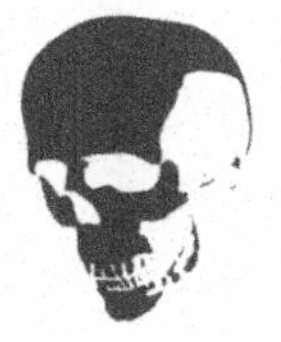

AND YOU

I can't keep being strong today,
I can't keep carrying this heavyweight.
I can't detach from the pain today,
I can't keep ignoring what is fake.
I have to stop.
I have to breathe.
I have to repair.
I have to get up off my knees.
I will carry on being strong today,
I will carry on carrying this heavyweight.
I will carry on feeling the pain today,
I will carry on accepting what is fake.
And you, you will not see any of this.

ATTENTION

Look at me,
not that me,
the real me,
the creature that craves your attention;
your glances,
your looks.
Talk to me,
hear me,
I have to feel your affections;
your gestures,
your touch.
Can you see it?
Can you feel it?
The gut-wrenching blackness,
the dankness of my soul,
it lies deep within;
tortured, alone.

AUTUMN LEAF

Like an autumn leaf devoid of life,
I lay here abandoned on the ground.
The crisp memories of my wasted summer
blowing through my remains.
Laying here I think of spring,
energy, life, pumping through me,
feeding my growth, spurring me on.
Touched, held, admired.
But now I lay here,
wasting away.
Motionless, untouched, ignored,
hoping for one final autumn breeze.
But tomorrow brings winter,
With frost, we fade.
And as any autumn leaf knows,
tomorrow we all turn to mulch.

AWAKEN

And as I close my eyes,
my arms wide open waiting for sleep.
I feel the warmth of her embrace,
the gentleness of her touch,
the soothing of her caress.
The brutal, painful, piercing
memories of my deceased parents.
And I am dragged back out,
into the darkness of the bedroom.
Heart racing and hurting,
yearning for sleep again,
knowing she will not return so willingly.

CLOSE

Here we stand
On the beach
Side by side
Out of reach

Close to touch
Oceans apart
Nothing between us
Broken hearts

Here we stand
Pain like a knife
In the place
I took my life

CRAWL

Crawling out of bed, I slip into my life.
Comfortable in its feel, yet heavy in its wear.
Straighten my broken back, damaged from the weight.
Stumble, mumble through the doorway,
another day too dark to bare.
Fuel the furnace, Stoke the fire.
Slow to start, give it time.
A warm embrace, a fragment of hope,
"Are you ok?"
I pause, I whisper, I choke, "I'll be fine..."

DISSAPEAR

This is a place you come to disappear,
a place you come to scream but no one hears.
Your pain, your misery for all to see,
no one here will echo your plea.
Contact, understanding, equality,
but your ego obscures reality.
Again you're just a passing face,
soon forgotten, gone without a trace.

DONKEY

When you carry everything
And everyone,
it's always the smallest thing
that breaks your back.
When you hold it all in
and don't let it show,
it's always the ones we love
that will feel the blow.
Share the weight,
share the pain,
suffering in darkness
you have nothing to gain.

MISERY LOVES COMPANY

Fingertips pushed deep inside,
squeezed in a vice-like grip.
The tension of failure,
anxiety leaks drip, drip, drip.
Memories I try to bury,
push them further down.
Hide them beneath the embarrassment,
never to be found.
I feel the pressure build up inside,
I try to escape from it through my phone.
No matter how hard I try,
it is the worst time I feel so alone.
When depression sinks its teeth in,
this might be the advice you seek.
Surround yourself with loved ones,
because misery loves company.

NO ONE

My world ceases to exist,
when you close your eyes.
I fade from existence,
when you turn your back.
I become the shadows,
when you turn away.
I am no one again,
when you say goodbye.

SIMPLE ACT OF KINDNESS

A simple act of kindness,
can change a person's day.
That moment you reach out
and tell them it's ok.
To us, they seem happy,
smiling, laugh along.
But people hide the pain beneath,
undercover from the strong.
So be kind and flash a smile,
be polite to others through life.
Because those simple acts of kindness
can stop so many suicides.

PART II
DISTURBED

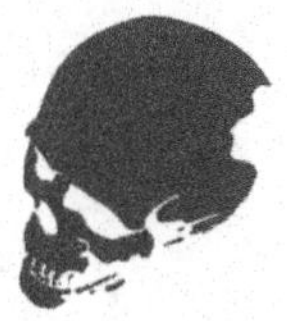

BIN BAG

Scrape me off the floor,
I can't do this anymore.
Crushing head-on impact,
split between the cracks.
Broken slabs where I lay,
motionless and on display.
Shovelled into bin bags,
blood splatters the slabs.
Stained on school kids minds,
like my brain matter, left behind.

BORN OF BLOOD

Love conquers all,
every demon subdued.
The worlds rage is tamed,
there was nothing for you to choose.
We believed in true love,
it was love at first sight.
We were soul mates,
but you loved a fight.
We had a sacred unholy love
it was superior and free.
I watched you every minute,
but you didn't love me.
So I gave you the ultimate gift,
it was life's final prize.
I sealed you within,
and I watched the flames rise.
If I couldn't have you,
I made sure nobody could.
The police didn't understand
that our love was born in blood.

BREATH

"Freeze," she said,
"Don't speak," she said,
"Accept," she said
"Wait," she said,
"Wait," she said,
"Wait".
"Sleep," she said,
"Silent," she said.
"Now!" she said,
"Blood!" she said,
"Again!" she said,
"Again!" she said,
"Run!" she said,
"Run!".
"Free," she said,
"Breath," she said,
"Breath"

COLD

I don't know what was so special about that night.
Was it the clouded, vacant stare in your eyes?
Was it the moonshine that danced on your pale blue skin?
Was it your mouth that had a slight grin that I thought was
charming?
Or your touch, cold and stiff, just the way I like it?
No,
I remember now,
you were my first,
my always,
you were my birth.

CREEP

I scurry away,
back under the floor, I go.
I will keep out of the way,
lost in my world of darkness below.
I hide in the shadows,
silent and out of reach.
I wait for your slumber,
so I can, beneath you, creep.
I bide my time,
watch your movements above,
and when you leave
I sneak out to smell your love.

DEVOUR

I pull you in closer,
you feel safe, secure.
Trusting like a calf to slaughter,
innocent, weak and pure.

I push back your hair
and trace the vain beneath your skin.
The arousal, hunger, urgency,
I hold you tighter and breath you in.

Slowly, I release the demon.
My canines start to grow,
I pierce your flesh, warm, sweet,
as your life begins to flow.

I feel your body grow heavy
as you feed my insatiable hunger.
Your heart slows down, stops,
to welcome the eternal slumber.

DIG

3 am.

Here I lie,

watching the shadows creep on to the ceiling.

The same questions keep churning in my head.

"Did I lock the door?"

"Did I turn off the lights?"

"Did I pay that bill?"

"Did I forget my gloves?"

"Did I dig deep enough?"

"Did I cover my tracks?"

"Did that car follow me?"

Then I hear the door downstairs creak open.

"Damn, I didn't dig deep enough."

DISSOLVE RESOLVE

I dissolve into your mind
through the smallest gap, I can find.
Underneath your skin, I crawl
an itch you can't control.
Whisper to your soul
poison your whole world.
Make you want to believe
trust my lies you're so naive.
But now the time has come,
I walk away I've had my fun,
you're left shattered, broken, won't mend.
You grab the knife
you want revenge.

DRAINED

She traces her nail down the vain in his neck,
riding the raised stream,
feeling his body heat grow.
The hairs on his neck awaken,
a cold shiver runs down his spine.
She traces the vain back up his neck, slowly.
Pushing her sharpened nail forward slightly, quickly,
and a thin red line flashes across his neck.
Blood fills the cut, the smell, the racing heart.
She licks his neck and life touches her tongue,
her excitement immediately rages.
Teeth expand, he flinches,
but she too quick and she drinks.
Fighting for his life,
pushing, lashing out.
Sucking, gulping.
But it's too late,
his heart slows, stops.
She drops him, and she leaves.
Leaving him Motionless, still,
drained,
dead.

FALL

Time speeds
Deep breaths
Ice cold
View widens
Eyes down
Drop below
Time slows
Knees buckle
Free fall
No return
Life floods
Heart stops

FLOORBOARDS

The squeaking of the turning screw,
awakens me from my sleep.
The floorboards get pulled back,
and daylight makes my eyes weak.
You stroke my cheek with your warm fingers,
arousing my icy skin.
You embrace me in your loving arms,
another night of unholy sin.
I know my time with you will be short,
and time flys when you're dead.
But, as long as I have your necro love,
my grave will be your bed.

GODFORSAKEN

Crippling, crippling, crippling cries
A man so strong yet love denied.
Damned, damned, the dam has broken
Soul ripped apart, sorrow woken.
Grasping, grasping, reaching out
Godforsaken, forever devout.
Belief, belief, believe in hate
Evil breeds, controls his fate.

HATED EVERYTHING

I'm the square peg forcing my way in,
the sheep in wolf's clothing.
I'm the fatness against the thin,
the wasp and the sting.
I'm the tonic with no gin,
the pat on the back for the win.
I'm the lottery ticket in the bin,
I'm your hated fucking everything.

HOW DO I LOVE THEE?

How do I love thee?
Let me count the ways.
Is it through the softness of my kiss?
Or the piercing of my blade?
Oh, my love,
How do I express thy desire for thee?
Is it through my touch, my lust,
Or by the slit throat of misery?

JULIA MITCH

Julia Mitch became a powerful witch,
developing her powers only for revenge.
All the ones who had done her wrong,
all the loser, cheating, scumbag men.
Hunting each one down one by one,
they wish they had never been born.
Flesh-eating, pustules of acidic fluid,
oozing from every cracked, blistering pore.
So, the moral of this poem is to be careful who you love,
for the ones who you do wrong and refer to as a bitch,
may one day come looking for you and take revenge,
as an angry malevolent fucked up, WITCH!

LIKE SUBSCRIBE

Come and watch me bleed,
drool over my imploding soul.
Wrenching from my failures,
to entertain you is my goal.
Feel my darkest hour
my suffering is pure,
no second-hand sickness here
there is no room for a cure.
Mentally drained, emotionally stained,
I volunteer my suffering pride,
Mock my internal death
But don't forget to like and subscribe.

THE MURDER OF MARY

Black, silent, perched,
they sit, watching.
Watching, the man, creep from behind and embrace her.
Watching, the man slit her throat, with his hand on her mouth
to stop her screams.
Watching, her loosely slump to the ground.
Watching, the frost on the ground melt,
from the warmth of her blood.
Watching, the man, learn over and lovingly close her eyelids.
Watching, him slowly, walk away.
They sit, watching.
Black, silent, perched.
A murder of crows,
watching the murder of Mary.

SAW

The flesh tears,
backwards and forwards the saw goes.
The blood flows,
the porcelain tiles are soaked.
The bath fills,
the body glides,
Teflon slide,
banging on the sides of the bath.
Blade meets bone,
and splinters churn.
Backwards and forwards the saw goes.

SKINDEEP

They say that beauty is only skin deep,
and it's what's on the inside that glows.
But I don't believe that for a minute,
beauty is only as deep as my knife goes.
For me, it's not about your weight,
or whether your hair is black or red.
There is nothing more beautiful
than to see you as a victim of our bloodshed.
I take pride in what I do,
I'm an artist, a connoisseur.
The hammer is my favourite tool
as I paint a masterpiece that you deplore.
You obsess with why I create
And what drove me to bring on this onslaught.
Yet as the police chase their tales
I will continue killing until caught.

SOMETHING

Excuse me World,
can I have your attention, please?
I have something to show you,
it's not something you will believe.
I have something buried deep inside,
it's something stronger than rage.
It's anger I can't control,
it's anger I cannot cage.
I have a feeling that if I let go
if I give in to its demands.
It's something that will rip through me
it will eat up our beautiful land.
It will cause carnage to this country,
Its darkness will devour all.
Its evil will eradicate everything
it will bring the end, it will not fall.
But for now, I will sit in silence,
and wait for it to subside.
For the evil that sits inside me,
will bring an end to all humankind.

STATIC

The old white transistor radio sits silently.
The dust gathers from years of neglect.
His hands wipe the ageing clear,
and his fingers turn the dial, silence, he expects.
But, the static crackles quietly at first,
and his heart gives a leap, rejoice!
And as he turns it up and tries to tune it in,
the only thing he hears is his dead, fathers voice.

PART III
PANDEMIC

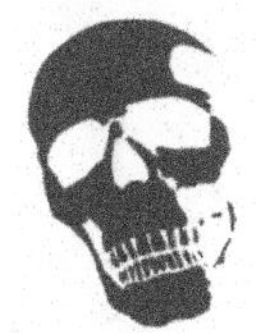

FUTURE BOY

I laughed out loud when he told me
The boy from the future
About the lockdown
the world shutdown

"Of course!" I mocked and went to slap his arm
He flinched and moved
Stepped back in shock
"Keep your distance, stop!"

He told me of the healthcare
Of all the deaths
The isolation
The destruction

He told me it was coming
And we won't see it till it was too late
"Don't be daft,
it will be 2020, not 1908!"

He told me of the call of arms
The volunteers
The love and gratitude
And also the idiotic attitudes

He told me everything
And that this was a warning
It won't end in the humans annihilations
But love, understanding and unity of the nations.

A NEW YEAR

Well, it is now 2021,
let us pray for the best year for everyone.
There is a lot of work to do,
especially for us who are growing food.
I know 2020 was a bag of manure for most and hopefully,
with the vaccine, we will eventually be over the worst.
We say goodbye to the loved ones we lost,
their lives to remember at all cost.
Now embrace the change and raise a glass,
to new beginnings and here's to kicking 2020 in the ass.

PANDEMIC

I went outside today
to face the abandoned familiarity.
The distance was obvious the trust was less,
the stupid ones ignoring the loneliness.
I watch my touch,
tried not to linger,
not knowing who did what to the ginger.
Head off to the register,
to make the contactless contractual buy.
I waited my turn in my 2-metre zone,
hoping that Covid-19 would fuck off and die.

PART IV
LIFE

FEEL

It entered my life today,
tore a hole in my world,
made me feel sick,
made me feel.

I wasn't expecting it at all,
I didn't see it coming,
made me feel dizzy,
made me feel.

I see how it got in now,
I didn't follow the instructions, left the door wide open,
made me feel alone,
made me feel.

I'm glad that this has happened,
I'm happy I was infected,
made me feel whole,
made me feel,

love.

HUMANS

The world is full of
amazing,
beautiful,
miraculous,
wonders that make you feel the true meaning of nature.

The breathtaking images that are out there,
the views,
the sights,
the feelings,
all that would bring anyone to tears.

Then there's humans...

HURT

When I was young,
I realised, just how many bad things,
outside,
could hurt me.
Now I'm older
I realise, just how many bad things,
inside,
can hurt me more.

OLDER

Another year passes by,
another grey hair to add to the collection of white.
Another picture to remind you of the event,
another day wasted, now forgot how it was misspent.
Another cake to remind you of your waist,
another set of candles to burn away.
Another birthday fades into the past,
another year as your age grows fast.

ROCK STAR

When I was a teen,
before my life had travelled far.
I wanted to be a metal musician,
upon a stage, a long-haired rock star.

I listen to all the music,
I went to see the bands live.
I grew my hair, wore the clothes
learned to play, it was my way of life.

Even though my life was good,
it's a shame my talents were not.
I settled into working life
and worked on what I had got.

Now years later, no hair, family
and a steady full-time job.
My goals have changed, I'm an author now,
and my dream is to be a book rock god!

SIRENS SONG

Lost in a sea of anger and hate,
I am waiting for you to come.
A soul of kindness and love,
reaching out to everyone.
Their words find your eyes,
and you see their unconditional light.
Absorbing their loneliness,
you know they won't put up a fight.
They react to your requests,
drip feeding your ego.
Desperate humans pleading,
so drawn in, they can't let go.
But I'm no different to them
your sirens song is irresistible.
You don't know who the fuck I am,
to you I'm invisible.

SLEEP

Struggling to
Lose myself in the
Envelope of
Eternal
Paralyses

STORIES

Stories of life,
of worlds,
of deaths,
of births,
of love,
of hate,
of adventure,
of fate.
Life's bound together
over shifts of time and place,
across the expansion,
of this old wooden bookcase.

TEENAGE MIND

My mind thinks it's younger than what it is.
My mind thinks it's still a fucking kid.
My brain tells it no,
that it has to let go.
But now it's sulking,
locked itself in its bedroom,
and now it's churning out poetry that makes no sense to
anyone!

PART V
STRENGTH

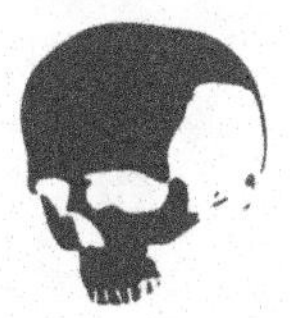

BETTER THAN YOU

I wasn't always together,
I wasn't always calm.
I had my fair share of being bullied,
they always kept me down.

A little insult here,
the odd kick there.
Nothing too serious,
not that the teachers cared.

Never had a jacket,
always cold.
Didn't have the right trainers,
clothes were too old.

But then things changed,
and I got seen.
People got jealous,
they couldn't believe.

I started to realise,
that I was more.
The bastards couldn't stand it,
they cut me on the floor.

Thirty years later,
I see what's true,
You fucking pricks didn't like me,
because I was always better than you.

DAZZLE

Don't look at them,
don't pay attention,
you don't need to see it,
your talent is special.
Don't listen to it,
don't let it in,
the imposter won't win,
you are your arts vessel.
Embrace your madness.
Embrace your dark.
Embrace your silence.
Blind the world with your spark.

GROW THROUGH

One day I planted a seed,
I sat and watched it germinate.
I watered and fed it
and I filled it with hate.

When it raised its shoots
and started to grow.
I tried to stop it,
I didn't want it anymore.

I pushed it back,
tried to stomp it down.
But the branches crept through
and dominated the ground.

Eventually, I gave up,
I have bowed to the powers.
It now has a voice,
and we have a field of flowers.

Inner beauty will always shine through in the end.

KING OF RETRIBUTION

I am your enemy, your foe,
your lucid brutal dream.
Your blood dripping nightmare,
your silence when you scream.

I am your anxiety, your panic,
your pounding racing heart.
Your shadow when you walk,
your fear in the dark.

I am your anger, your rage,
your banging, full of hate.
Your stomping, your screaming,
your past and your fate.

I am your present, your now,
my revenge, prosecution.
You will be stopped and culled,
as I am the King of retribution.

NOTHING

I am nothing unique.
I create nothing new.
I have nothing special.
I am nothing to you.
I see nothing in my future.
I have nothing in my past.
I show nothing right now.
I believe nothing can last.
Nothing keeps me here.
Nothing wants me there.
Nothing reaches out for me.
But honestly, I don't care.

RISE

Up from the depth, it grows.
Pushing out,
searching,
breaking the surface.
Reach for the light,
to grow,
to feed,
to absorb.
A tendril holding,
curling,
climbing.
A flash of beauty,
flowering elegance.
Then the fruit of the labour,
sweetness,
encapsulated within.
Harvest,
then death.
A season has gone,
ready for the rebirth,
nature breaths again.

SHORT

Life is short.
Flash fiction.
Your story wrote on a stamp.
Time restriction.
But it's not about word counts,
or the ending as such.
But the loves, the lives,
and all the souls that you touch.

SWING THE AXE

Today I fell apart again,
another notch on my skin,
steel slivers crimson trace.
Another sledgehammer name,
another crippling blow,
another lying smile.
A promise of revenge to forget.
Friends retreat,
no angels to protect you.
Everyday hacks at you,
another chop from the axe,
another day to run.
Another place to hide,
to hate your life.
One day things will change,
one day I will get my revenge,
one day it will be my turn to swing the axe.

THE STATE

I grew up on a council estate in the '70s,
we stuck to our own, hated the other area's kids.
We'd get bored, knock on doors, run away quick.
We'd climb down drains, steal from shops and chase with shit
on a stick.
The local punks discovered glue,
that turned the area a creamy plastic hue.
We'd get chases from the psychopaths,
nothing serious just did it for a laugh.
Then came the teens, locked in our rooms, music loud,
Speccie's, Sega's, we avoided the high school crowd.
Now I'm older, grey, lines and mortgages,
I wish my kids didn't have to go through the same shit.
But they had their share of dickheads and that's what I hate,
regardless of what I do, I can't get off this god damn council
estate.

PART VI
LOSS

"Our dog of 14 years, so gentle but suffered so much when she was older. That moment we decided to do the kind thing, holding her whilst she was injected, feeling her life drain from her is something I still feel now ten years later."

NINA

I'm sorry that this has gone on for too long,
the pain that claws and chews.
You are not the same,
the pills have consumed you,
I wish I could start again and make you like new.

As I stand here,
I can feel your fear as I hold you in my arms.
Your unconditional love and total submission,
before the storm always comes the calm.

She unleashes the relief,
I un-leash my pain.
I feel your life fade away,
the horror and grief,
the instant regret.
I will never forget,
I will never forget,
I will never forget, today.

Please forgive me.

"Self explanatory really, losing my Dad ten years ago and Mum just a few months ago the scars are real. There is a moment where the death hits you, and it feels like someone just wringing every tear, every sob, as though you are removing your life essence. It hurts for so long and never really heals, you can only keep placing cheap plasters over the pain."

LOSS KILLS

Loss kills.
The soul is hurt so bad it's torn,
it's ripped from its being,
dragged,
scarred,
beaten,
and tossed back into its shell,
dying.
You carry the loss around forever,
till the day you rip someone's soul to shreds.
No one will live forever, but the loss will.
In time, it eases.
In time, you learn to cope.
In time, you lose again.
Loss kills.

"The last day of my father's life was heartbreaking to look back on. I visited him with my Mum on the evening, read some get well cards to him, told him Leeds had beaten Man United in the cup, he smiled. But then we left after a while. Later, I received a call informing me they believe it would be his last night. I thought he would be fine, and I would see him the day after. But they were right, and I wasn't with him when he died. The choices that we make."

LOST YOU

You lost the fight today.
You didn't have the strength to keep hold.
The daily drain took your last drop.
I wasn't brave.
I wasn't bold.
I know I left you and that will hurt,
I wasn't there in your coffin room as the mortal curtains
closed.
Our family has a hole in it,
your memories will leave us never,
but I'm sorry Dad,
I let you down, and that will stay with me forever.

"I always wanted to have a conversation with my Dad after his death. I always wondered what it would be like and this was my take on it, I think there would have been more complaining, but you get the gist."

DAD

I sat down and talked with my Dad tonight.
Words of wisdom,
years of experience,
odd comment of spite.
We had a drink you chose bitter - I had tea.
We talked about Mum, football and my family.
We laughed at the dogs and chatted about the latest gadgets.
You complained about the government, income and taxes.
I cried and changed the tone,
Then I realised you're still gone, and we're still alone.

"I wrote this a day after Mum had passed. I was angry that she
gave up, she stopped eating; she just stopped. We visited every
day. We held her hands whilst she drifted in and out, fighting.
Saying goodbye like that is hard, but we had said goodbye to
her so many times before we became accepting really. She got
the ending she wanted, and I am relieved for that.
I look back now, even though it tears a hole in me, I know this
is what she wanted. I know she and my dad will be on holiday
somewhere beautiful now. She did have a smile on her face
when she died."

MUM

Crushed by our loss,
your last word was spoken.
Your eyes closed forever,
our hearts lay broken.
Unbreakable bonds strained,
your last wish followed.
To watch you fade away,
it left us hollow.
Like a warrior, you fought to the end,
final strength in your frailty.
The time passed so quick,
yet it felt like an eternity.
But now you will be happy,
as you welcome death's embrace.
All your pain and anguish departed,
leaving us with a smile upon your face.

"Every Sunday, I would visit my mother in her care home, then when lockdown started, I would speak to her via Alexa as we couldn't visit. But every week we had the same conversations. Towards the end she got so mixed up and gave up, she just stopped, it killed me."

IN YOUR ROOM

It's five o'clock,
Sunday afternoon.
I call you up,
to speak to you in your room.
We chat about your week,
and you ask how we are all going.
How you got mixed up with the days,
That there's been no call, and you worried.
I ask if you have been up,
and got out of your room.
You say no,
but you promise you will do soon.
You ask about the silly things,
and you get angry because you can't remember.
Like your age, who you were,
what we look like, my father.
I say Covid will soon be over,
and I can come and see you.
It's not the same using this machine,
but at least it's getting us through.
Well, it's five o'clock again,
Sunday afternoon.
"Alexa, drop-in" Then I stop, I remember,
That you're gone, and there is someone else now sat waiting in
your room.

"I wrote this poem for my mothers funeral. It represented a time when life was simple, and we would go away in a family-sized frame tent, we did this as often as possible. I always yearn for the coast, and I think this is why. I miss you, Mum."

CANVAS POCKETS

Blossom covers the ground once again,
another spring fades into summer
and all we have are lost warm days.
The smell of bacon cooking under canvas,
BBQ sausages and half-cooked chicken
and we laugh under sun-rays in our camping chairs.
Evenings out and the smell of beer lingers,
warm nights by torchlight
And the smell of rubber air beds moving without control.
We had a good childhood, not perfect either,
but at least we have memories we can feel.
So thank you and safe journey,
until we meet again we will keep you tucked away,
safe inside,
our canvas pockets.

ABOUT THE AUTHOR

The author of Emotion Corrosion, Leigh Haddington, can be found lurking around Leeds, England. Husband and a father of two, most of his time is taken up with his full-time job and growing veg (not this has anything to do with his writing).

Raised on a diet of video nasties in the very early eighties, a teenage life of metal and horror films, with the drippings of horror books from King and Herbert, Leigh developed a twisted world that wouldn't look lost on an Alice Cooper album.

facebook.com/leighhaddington
twitter.com/leighhaddington
instagram.com/leigh.haddington

Kings of Hell

"Better to reign in Hell than serve in Heaven."

Lucifer in *Paradise Lost* by John Milton

Desperate to save her son's life, Jude Fitzroy, signs a contract with the devil. She gets to raise Nick until he is eighteen and then Lucifer will take his place - she will never know the difference, and Nick will rule Hell in Lucifer's stead.

A life swap with the King of Hell wasn't how Nick saw his future but the past had sealed his fate. Now, not only does he have power and magic beyond his wildest dreams, but also a life that is dragging him through his worst nightmares.

In a world where Hell is on the doorstep of everyone's life, Nick discovers just how far he will have to go for his family, freedom and a future of being himself. Lucifer, however, has other ideas and will do anything to keep the contract in place.

***

"A dark, fun ride into fiery depths."

Isaac Thorne

Author of The Gordon Place

"It's a book for those who don't mind a bit of slicing and dicing."

Dylan J Morgan

Author of Highland Cove